Layers of Learning

Year Two • Unit Twelve

Eastern Europe
Hungary
Metals
Printmaking

Published by HooDoo Publishing
United States of America
© 2014 Layers of Learning
Copies of maps or activities may be made for a particular family or classroom.
ISBN 978-1495314315

Units At A Glance: Topics For All Four Years of the Layers of Learning Program

1	History	Geography	Science	The Arts
1	Mesopotamia	Maps & Globes	Planets	Cave Paintings
2	Egypt	Map Keys	Stars	Egyptian Art
3	Europe	Global Grids	Earth & Moon	Crafts
4	Ancient Greece	Wonders	Satellites	Greek Art
5	Babylon	Mapping People	Humans in Space	Poetry
6	The Levant	Physical Earth	Laws of Motion	List Poems
7	Phoenicians	Oceans	Motion	Moral Stories
8	Assyrians	Deserts	Fluids	Rhythm
9	Persians	Arctic	Waves	Melody
10	Ancient China	Forests	Machines	Chinese Art
11	Early Japan	Mountains	States of Matter	Line & Shape
12	Arabia	Rivers & Lakes	Atoms	Color & Value
13	Ancient India	Grasslands	Elements	Texture & Form
14	Ancient Africa	Africa	Bonding	African Tales
15	First North Americans	North America	Salts	Creative Kids
16	Ancient South America	South America	Plants	South American Art
17	Celts	Europe	Flowering Plants	Jewelry
18	Roman Republic	Asia	Trees	Roman Art
19	Christianity	Australia & Oceania	Simple Plants	Instruments
20	Roman Empire	You Explore	Fungi	Composing Music

2	History	Geography	Science	The Arts
1	Byzantines	Turkey	Climate & Seasons	Byzantine Art
2	Barbarians	Ireland	Forecasting	Illumination
3	Islam	Arabian Peninsula	Clouds & Precipitation	Creative Kids
4	Vikings	Norway	Special Effects	Viking Art
5	Anglo Saxons	Britain	Wild Weather	King Arthur Tales
6	Charlemagne	France	Cells and DNA	Carolingian Art
7	Normans	Nigeria	Skeletons	Canterbury Tales
8	Feudal System	Germany	Muscles, Skin, & Cardiopulmonary	Gothic Art
9	Crusades	Balkans	Digestive & Senses	Religious Art
10	Burgundy, Venice, Spain	Switzerland	Nerves	Oil Paints
11	Wars of the Roses	Russia	Health	Minstrels & Plays
12	Eastern Europe	Hungary	Metals	Printmaking
13	African Kingdoms	Mali	Carbon Chem	Textiles
14	Asian Kingdoms	Southeast Asia	Non-metals	Vivid Language
15	Mongols	Caucasus	Gases	Fun With Poetry
16	Medieval China & Japan	China	Electricity	Asian Arts
17	Pacific Peoples	Micronesia	Circuits	Arts of the Islands
18	American Peoples	Canada	Technology	Indian Legends
19	The Renaissance	Italy	Magnetism	Renaissance Art I
20	Explorers	Caribbean Sea	Motors	Renaissance Art II

3	History	Geography	Science	The Arts
1	Age of Exploration	Argentina and Chile	Classification & Insects	Fairy Tales
2	The Ottoman Empire	Egypt and Libya	Reptiles & Amphibians	Poetry
3	Mogul Empire	Pakistan & Afghanistan	Fish	Mogul Arts
4	Reformation	Angola & Zambia	Birds	Reformation Art
5	Renaissance England	Tanzania & Kenya	Mammals & Primates	Shakespeare
6	Thirty Years' War	Spain	Sound	Baroque Music
7	The Dutch	Netherlands	Light & Optics	Baroque Art I
8	France	Indonesia	Bending Light	Baroque Art II
9	The Enlightenment	Korean Pen.	Color	Art Journaling
10	Russia & Prussia	Central Asia	History of Science	Watercolors
11	Conquistadors	Baltic States	Igneous Rocks	Creative Kids
12	Settlers	Peru & Bolivia	Sedimentary Rocks	Native American Art
13	13 Colonies	Central America	Metamorphic Rocks	Settler Sayings
14	Slave Trade	Brazil	Gems & Minerals	Colonial Art
15	The South Pacific	Australasia	Fossils	Principles of Art
16	The British in India	India	Chemical Reactions	Classical Music
17	Boston Tea Party	Japan	Reversible Reactions	Folk Music
18	Founding Fathers	Iran	Compounds & Solutions	Rococo
19	Declaring Independence	Samoa and Tonga	Oxidation & Reduction	Creative Crafts I
20	The American Revolution	South Africa	Acids & Bases	Creative Crafts II

4	History	Geography	Science	The Arts
1	American Government	USA	Heat & Temperature	Patriotic Music
2	Expanding Nation	Pacific States	Motors & Engines	Tall Tales
3	Industrial Revolution	U.S. Landscapes	Energy	Romantic Art I
4	Revolutions	Mountain West States	Energy Sources	Romantic Art II
5	Africa	U.S. Political Maps	Energy Conversion	Impressionism I
6	The West	Southwest States	Earth Structure	Impressionism II
7	Civil War	National Parks	Plate Tectonics	Post-Impressionism
8	World War I	Plains States	Earthquakes	Expressionism
9	Totalitarianism	U.S. Economics	Volcanoes	Abstract Art
10	Great Depression	Heartland States	Mountain Building	Kinds of Art
11	World War II	Symbols and Landmarks	Chemistry of Air & Water	War Art
12	Modern East Asia	The South States	Food Chemistry	Modern Art
13	India's Independence	People of America	Industry	Pop Art
14	Israel	Appalachian States	Chemistry of Farming	Modern Music
15	Cold War	U.S. Territories	Chemistry of Medicine	Free Verse
16	Vietnam War	Atlantic States	Food Chains	Photography
17	Latin America	New England States	Animal Groups	Latin American Art
18	Civil Rights	Home State Study	Instincts	Theater & Film
19	Technology	Home State Study II	Habitats	Architecture
20	Terrorism	America in Review	Conservation	Creative Kids

Unit 2-12

Printable Pack

This unit includes printables at the end. To make life easier for you we also created digital printable packs for each unit. To retrieve your printable pack for Unit 2-12, please visit

www.layers-of-learning.com/digital-printable-packs/

Put the printable pack in your shopping cart and use this coupon code:

7734UNIT2-12

Your printable pack will be free.

LAYERS OF LEARNING INTRODUCTION

This is part of a series of units in the Layers of Learning homeschool curriculum, including the subjects of history, geography, science, and the arts. Children from 1st through 12th can participate in the same curriculum at the same time – family school style.

The units are intended to be used in order as the basis of a complete curriculum (once you add in a systematic math, reading, and writing program). You begin with Year 1 Unit 1 no matter what ages your children are. Spend about 2 weeks on each unit. You pick and choose the activities within the unit that appeal to you and read the books from the book list that are available to you or find others on the same topic from your library. We highly recommend that you use the timeline in every history section as the backbone. Then flesh out your learning with reading and activities that highlight the topics you think are the most important.

Alternatively, you can use the units as activity ideas to supplement another curriculum in any order you wish. You can still use them with all ages of children at the same time.

When you've finished with Year One, move on to Year Two, Year Three, and Year Four. Then begin again with Year One and work your way through the years again. Now your children will be older, reading more involved books, and writing more in depth. When you have completed the sequence for the second time, you start again on it for the third and final time. If your student began with Layers of Learning in 1st grade and stayed with it all the way through she would go through the four year rotation three times, firmly cementing the information in her mind in ever increasing depth. At each level you should expect increasing amounts of outside reading and writing. High schoolers in particular should be reading extensively, and if possible, participating in discussion groups.

☺ ☺ ☺ These icons will guide you in spotting activities and books that are appropriate for the age of child you are working with. But if you think an activity is too juvenile or too difficult for your kids, adjust accordingly. The icons are not there as rules, just guides.

☺ GRADES 1-4

☺ GRADES 5-8

☺ GRADES 9-12

Within each unit we share:
- EXPLORATIONS, activities relating to the topic;
- EXPERIMENTS, usually associated with science topics;
- EXPEDITIONS, field trips;
- EXPLANATIONS, teacher helps or educational philosophies.

In the sidebars we also include Additional Layers, Famous Folks, Fabulous Facts, On the Web, and other extra related topics that can take you off on tangents, exploring the world and your interests with a bit more freedom. The curriculum will always be there to pull you back on track when you're ready.

You can learn more about how to use this curriculum at www.layers-of-learning.com/layers-of-learning-program/

UNIT TWELVE
EASTERN EUROPE – HUNGARY – METALS – PRINTMAKING

A mind without instruction can no more bear fruit than can a field, however fertile, without cultivation.
-Cicero, Roman Statesman

	LIBRARY LIST:
HISTORY	Search for: Lithuania, Poland, Bulgaria, Serbia, Hungary, Eastern European History, Teutonic Knights . . . we couldn't find many kids books on these subjects, rely on <u>The Usborne Encyclopedia of World History</u> and <u>The Kingfisher History of the World</u>. 😊 😊 <u>Hidden Tales From Eastern Europe</u> by Antonia Barber. 😊 <u>The White Stag</u> by Kate Seredy. Tells the legendary tale of the Hun and Magyar migration to the land that is now Hungary. Makes a great read aloud. 😊 <u>The Trumpeter of Krakow</u> by Eric P. Kelly. Historical novel based on true events of the 15th century. 😊 😊 <u>Teutonic Knight: 1190-1561</u> by David Nicolle. Heavily illustrated. 😊 😊 <u>Tannenberg 1410: Disaster for the Teutonic Knights</u> by Stephen Turnbull. 😊 <u>Poland: A History</u> by Adam Zamoyski. A thousand years of Polish history in a readable single volume. 😊 <u>A Concise History of Bulgaria</u> by R.J. Crampton. 😊 <u>The Hungarians: A Thousand Years of Victory in Defeat</u> by Paul Lendvai. 😊 <u>The Northern Crusades</u> by Eric Christiansen.
GEOGRAPHY	Search for: Hungary 😊 😊 😊 <u>One Time Dog Market at Buda and Other Hungarian Folk Tales</u> by Irma Molnar, trans. 😊 😊 😊 <u>How To Draw Hungary's Sights and Symbols</u> by Betsy Dru Tecco. Part of a series. Cement the country and culture of Hungary in your mind by drawing famous icons of this land. 😊 😊 😊 <u>Over a Bridge: A Kid's Guide to Budapest, Hungary</u> by Penelope Dyan. 😊 <u>Little Rooster's Diamond Button</u> by Margaret Read MacDonald. A retelling of a Hungarian fairy tale. Magical regurgitating roosters and evil kings . . . Also look for <u>The Valiant Red Rooster</u> by Eric Kimmel, it's the same story told differently. 😊 😊 <u>The Good Master</u> by Kate Seredy. Young Jancsi and his cousin Kate grow up on a Hungarian farm in the early 20th century. 😊 😊 <u>The Singing Tree</u> by Kate Seredy. Jancsi and Kate have to grow up quickly when Father is called to go to the Great War. 😊 😊 <u>The Fall of the Red Star</u> by Helen M. Szablya. Novel set during the 1956 Hungarian revolution vs Russia. Intense, should create good discussions with your kids. 😊 😊 <u>The Handbook of the New Eastern Europe</u> by Michael Kort. History & politics to the year 2000.

SCIENCE	Search for: metals 😊 🌐 <u>Metal</u> by Claire Llewellen 😊 🌐 <u>Copper</u> by Salvatore Tocci 😊 🌐 <u>Gold </u> by Salvatore Tocci. Look for other metals in this series. Lead, zinc, and more. 🌐 <u>Metals and the Environment</u> by Kathryn Whyman 😊 🌐 <u>Metal</u> by Chris Oxlade. 😊 <u>Metals and Metalloids</u> by Monica Halka, PhD.
THE ARTS	Search for: printmaking, you may find sections on the history of printmaking in large art anthologies; many art project idea books also include a section on printmaking 😊 🌐 😊 <u>Cool Printmaking: The Art of Creativity for Kids!</u> by Anders Hanson. A project book with lots of fun printmaking ideas. 😊 🌐 😊 <u>Art Lab For Kids: 52 Creative Adventures in Drawing, Painting, Printmaking, Paper, and Mixed Media for Budding Artists</u> by Susan Schwake. This art project book only has a few printmaking projects, but it's a fun resource book with lots of ideas. 😊 🌐 😊 <u>Print and Stamp Lab: 52 Ideas for Handmade Upcycled Printing Tools</u> by Traci Bunkers. 😊 🌐 😊 <u>The History of Printmaking</u> by Scholastic Books. 😊 🌐 😊 <u>Nature Printing: 30 Projects for Creating Beautiful Prints, Wearables, and Home Furnishings</u> by Laura Donnelly Bethmann. 🌐 😊 <u>Print Workshop: Hand Printing Techniques and Truly Original Projects</u> by Christine Schmidt.

HISTORY: EASTERN EUROPE

Additional Layer

Why do history books talk so much about battles?

Think about the effect a battle can have on the course of history. What if the Golden Horde had defeated Lithuania at the battle of Blue Waters (see image), taken Kiev instead, and proceeded to attack Estonia, Finland, Poland and Germany?

Can you name some battles that would have changed the course of history if they had gone the other way?

Fabulous Fact

Hungary is located in the Carpathian Basin, a fertile valley surrounded by mountain ranges including the Carpathians, Alps, Dinarc Alps, and Balkans. The Danube River runs through the basin, cutting it nearly in two. Sometimes this basin is called Pannonian, a name that came from the Roman name for this territory.

During the early middle ages, while Europe was still very unstable following the fall of Rome, tribes from Asia in the east began to migrate in, making war on the Christians already living in the area. Eventually these new tribes settled down and made kingdoms of their own. Many of the kingdoms lasted only a short time, but a few became the basis of modern eastern European countries. Those that became permanent eventually adopted the Christianity of those they had conquered.

Battle of Blue Waters between Lithuania and the Golden Horde in 1362. Lithuania wins, solidifying their hold on Kiev, and keeping the Golden Horde out of Northern Europe.

The main states that emerged from all the chaos were Poland, Hungary, Lithuania, Serbia, Bulgaria, and the lands of the Teutonic Knights, who took over Prussia. Meanwhile the Russians, who had been expanding and solidifying their power as well, were being attacked by the Mongols from Asia also. The Russians became a vassal state of the Mongols. Later the Mongols would move further into Europe, threatening the fragile political systems in place and creating an environment where feudalism flourished.

At the same time the Mongols were pushing in from the east, the Seljuk Turks were pushing up from the south. The Turks conquered the Byzantines piece by piece and then proceeded to make war on the Serbian, Bulgarian, and Hungarian kingdoms.

☺ ☺ ☺ EXPLORATION: Timeline

You can find printable timeline squares at the end of this unit.

- 895 Magyars begin to settle Carpathian Basin
- 955 Germans beat Magyar invaders, pope creates Holy Roman Empire
- 1001 Pope recognizes Christian Kingdom of Hungary, Stephen is king
- 1212 Golden Bull founds Kingdom of Bohemia
- 1217 Serbian Kingdom proclaimed and established
- 1224-1239 Teutonic Knights conquer Prussians
- 1237 Mongols begin to invade Russia
- 1241 Mongols invade Poland and Hungary
- 1242 Russians defeat Teutonic Knights at Lake Peipus
- 1342 Death of Gedymin, founder of Lithuania
- 1355-1378 Charles IV of Bohemia reigns as Holy Roman Emperor
- 1362 Battle of Blue Waters, Lithuanians beat the Golden Horde, giving Lithuania control over Kiev
- 1386 Poland and Lithuania united through marriage
- 1389 Battle of Kosovo, Ottomans defeat and control Balkans
- 1410 Teutonic Knights defeated at the battle of Tannenberg (Grunwald) by a Polish-Lithuanian alliance
- 1526 Ottomans defeat Hungarians at the Battle of Mohacs and then begin to occupy much of eastern Europe

A painting depicting the aftermath of the Battle of Tannenberg. After the battle most of the leadership of the Teutonic knights lay dead on the field. They never recover their former power and Lithuania and Poland become powerhouses in the region.

Famous Folks

Alexander Nevsky is a saint in the Greek Orthodox church. He was the prince of Novgorod and a military leader who had significant victories over the Finns and the Swedes, but he also had to pay tribute to the Golden Horde.

Read more about him.

Additional Layer

One of the things that distinguished eastern Europe from western Europe anciently was that the east was influenced by Greek culture, including Byzantium, while the west was influenced more by the Latin culture of Rome.

Think about some of the differences between Greek and Roman philosophy, government, and religion. Even the alphabets are different.

Famous Folks

Mary I of Hungary succeeded her father as ruler of Hungary in September 1382. As she was a minor, her mother, Elizabeth, ruled as her regent.

She was married to Sigismund of Luxembourg in 1385. Later that year she was deposed by Charles, a relative who was in the male line. Just a few months later Mary invited dear cousin Charles to her estate and had him stabbed to death. She retook the throne but shortly was captured by her political enemies along with her mother Elizabeth. Elizabeth was murdered, but Mary was freed by her husband. She ruled with her husband until her death.

Fabulous Fact

The ancient name of the Hungarians is Magyar.

☺ ☺ ☺ EXPLORATION: Eastern European Kingdoms

Use the Eastern Europe map from the end of this unit. Label and then color the Eastern European Kingdoms.

None of these "countries" were like our modern nations politically. They were more often loose collections of tiny kingdoms and city states. Often the local barons had complete control with only nominal input from the monarch of the region. When you see the borders of Russia on the map, do not assume that it was one united nation. It was not. Though there was some control exerted from Kiev, the ties were much more to the local ruler than to a centralized state. The local rulers paid tribute to Kiev. Also the map shows only a few of the most important cities. In reality, the land was fairly densely populated and full of towns and cities. Castles and fortresses dotted the land and farms stretched across the plains and near the rivers. These were cosmopolitan, sophisticated people who traded across Europe, the Middle East, and North Africa, not backwoods rural people.

HUNGARY

😊 🟢 **EXPLORATION: Magyar Artisans**

The Hungarian nation was settled between 895 and 902 AD. Previous to this time they had been a series of separate tribes of wandering nomads without a homeland. They wanted a permanent home, but as individual tribes were never strong enough to defeat anyone and to take good land. There is lots of available uninhabited land in the world, even today, but the stuff left isn't all that great for farming and living. It's either too dry or too cold or too something. The Hungarians were finally united under a guy named Arpad and he led them to the Carpathian Basin, a fertile valley in the midst of the Carpathian Mountains. The Hungarians weren't satisfied even then though, and for years they were the scourge of Europe, successfully conquering and raiding as far west as Spain. Finally they were beaten by the German King Otto I at the Battle of Lechfield in 955, and that put an end to their raiding in the west, though they kept harassing the Byzantines for decades after.

What we know about the early Hungarians, called Magyars, comes mostly from accounts of their enemies and from their graves. The picture below is of an ornamental end of a horse strap found in a grave of a rich man. The ornament is made of silver and gold and has a picture of a stag bounding away. Their art was all done to decorate useful items, like most other ancient people (and modern people too). Though the Magyars were nomads, they were skilled artisans, used a written runic language, and were wealthy.

You can color the picture of the stag strap end from the end of this unit, cut it out, and paste it to cardboard. Then attach the cardboard to a piece of cloth, like a strap, to see how it would have looked.

We know the Magyars were nomadic and lived in Yurts on the steppes of Central Asia. They are possibly descended from Mesopotamian people, but scholars squabble a great deal over their true origins. We also know they were brilliant horsemen and that is why they were such a scourge across Europe. The horse made them quick, maneuverable, and bigger – more formidable in battle. Their ancient tales tell of a magical white stag that guided their ancestor, Arpad, to the fertile lands Carpathian Basin. Can you see these parts of their history in the strap from a horse harness?

Famous Folks

King Matthias Corvinus ruled Hungary from 1458 at the age of 14 until his death in 1490.

He was the first European monarch to adopt the Italian Renaissance philosophies. He encouraged education and the arts and tried to rule as Plato's philosopher king. He is known in Hungary as "the Just."

Matthias, like all other early Hungarian kings, was elected. His dad was John Hunyadi, a very influential and much loved Hungarian noble. Read about him in a sidebar on the next page.

Additional Layer

Hungary is rich in land, gold, silver, and salt, all which made it a very wealthy and powerful state until World War I.

Additional Layer

In Hungary in 1222, King Andrew II was forced by his nobles to sign the Golden Bull. It mandated that nobles be treated equally and fairly under the law and made it legal for nobles to disobey the king if he was in violation of the law. Some say the Golden Bull was influenced by the Magna Charta.

Famous Folks

John Hunyadi was a powerful Hungarian noble who led the war effort against the invading Ottoman Turks in the 1440's and 50's. He is a folk hero among Hungarians today.

☺ ☻ EXPLORATION: Saint Stephen

Always the kingdom had passed down to the eldest living male member of the family. Tradition stated that it was so. Always the people had worshiped the old pagan gods, and always the people had had their ancient rights as free men.

King Geza converted to Christianity and desired to be more like the west and convert his people to his own faith so he taught his son, Vajk, of his desires and ordered that Vjak be the next king of the Hungarians, though the rightful successor was Geza's brother, not his son. Following Geza's death, wars tore the nation apart as the two sides vied for power. Vajk, was married to Gisselle, a German princess, and brought his German mercenaries to the battle. While Uncle Koppany brought his Magyar tribesmen. At the time the people saw it as a war between the Germans and the Magyars, but it was actually much more personal than that.

Make a chart showing what they were fighting for:

Vajk	Uncle Koppany
Christianity (by the sword if necessary)	Old pagan ways (and freedom of religion)
Western values (feudalism and Roman Catholicism)	Byzantine influences
Change to Latin language	Retain runic alphabet
Tribes subjugated to the crown	Tribes retain semi-autonomous state
Eldest son inherits the throne, Divine Right	Eldest prince inherits throne, ancient custom

Turns out Vjak won, changed his name to Stephen (his baptismal name) to sound more western, converted his people with missionaries and by the sword when necessary, instituted a feudal system, changed the official language to Latin, and broke off all ties with Byzantium. For his pains he was named a saint by the Catholic Church and we know him as Saint Stephen I. His reign marks the beginning of a peasant class in Hungary and the beginning of Hungary as a nation instead of a loose collection of Magyar tribes.

☺ ☻ EXPLORATION: Saint Stephen's Crown

There is no doubt that Stephen was a devout Christian. He is held in great esteem by the people of Hungary. They celebrate a national holiday on August 20th honoring him. They have his right hand they keep and revere. Yes, it's his real right hand. If you have a taste for the macabre and want to see it there are pictures online, just search for "The Holy Right".

The crown of Hungary is also reputed to be descended from Stephen. A crown blessed and given to him by officials in the Catholic Church and recognizing him as a Christian king was held in Stephen's hand as he lay dying. He held the crown aloft and declared that the holy crown was the king and the Holy Mother (Mary, mother of Jesus) was the Queen.

Hungarians do not crown their king. Their Crown is their king and they look for someone's head to put it on.

Make a paper representation of the Hungarian crown. Use construction paper or poster board. Spray paint it gold. Use strings and beads to make the tassels that hang from the rim. Use pipe cleaners to make the cross at the top.

☻ ☺ EXPLORATION: Defend Your Kingdom

Imagine that you are the monarch of a small nation surrounded by menacing neighbors. How would you protect your borders? Draw a map of your imaginary kingdom and your defense strategy. Discuss your options and plans with a group.

On The Web

It will probably be difficult to find books on eastern Europe and Hungary in the English language. www.hungarianhistory.com has many books on Hungary compiled and distributed for free on the web.

Fabulous Fact

All medieval Hungarian monarchs were descended from Árpád, the tribal Grand Prince who first the led the Magyar tribes across the Carpathian Mountains and conquered the Basin, making it their homeland.

Additional Layer

After Stephen I imposed Roman Catholicism on Hungary, future monarchs followed his example. They took measures to force people into the faith of Rome. Daughters of Muslims had to marry Christians. Jews could not be nobles or hold positions at court. Christians could not be subject to Muslims or Jews. There were extra taxes if you were of the wrong faith and members of the Orthodox church lost their noble titles and land, especially in Transylvania.

Here is what the Hungarians did:
1. Invite certain peoples to come in and act as border guards with the condition that they get special privileges.
2. Build forts and castles along the borders.
3. Fortify your churches to make them into fortresses in every town. Train some of the townspeople in defense.

One of the groups the Hungarians invited in for defense were the newly created Teutonic Knights. The Teutons were given lands, and they built castles along the border. They were tough and mean and well trained. They also became a little scary to the Hungarian King, Andrew III, who had invited them in the first place. He kicked them back out of Hungary before they could take his throne and the Teutons then went to Prussia where they stormed and pillaged and forced Christianity by the sword.

☺ ☻ EXPLORATION: Ruling at Home
Transylvania was an important and powerful duchy on the eastern edge of Hungary during the Middle Ages. It was ordered into three parts for each of the three nations who lived there. The Hungarians and ethnic Romanians lived in the Royal Counties. They were ruled by a few powerful Hungarian nobles who had private armies and castles. The rest of the people were serfs.

Transylvania
In Hungary During the Middle Ages

Szekely Seats — Royal Counties — Saxon Seats

The Szekely Seats were a specific tribe of Hungarians or perhaps cousins to the Hungarians. They protected the borders of Hungary. In exchange they were given autonomy, the right to rule themselves, and there were no serfs, just free landholders and free townsmen who ruled themselves.

The Saxon Seats had a similar arrangement. They had been enticed to move to Hungary from Germany in order for Hungary to have more skilled artisans (remember all their people were serfs) and more soldiers to defend the borders. In exchange the Saxons were promised autonomy. They had no serfs either and the people governed themselves.

To make their arrangement formal and to coordinate their defense, the leaders of the three Transylvanian peoples made a pact called the *Unio Trium Nationum*, The Union of the Three Nations, in 1438.

The majority of the people in the Hungarian controlled areas were Romanian in ethnicity and were never given any political power. The *Unio Trium Nationum* formalized this situation as well, and this arrangement lasted until after World War I. One of the provisos of the pact said that the two seats would come to the aid of the Hungarian nobles in case of serf uprisings. The serfs did revolt (more than once) and the seats did come to the aid of the nobility, but still, over the years the serfs gained more and more freedoms.

If you were the monarch or the duke how would you deal with irate peasants and a subjugated people? What laws and practices would you enact? Remember, you have to keep your nobles happy too and they have private armies. A king cannot do just whatever he wants. Would you keep the peasants down with your soldiers? Would you give in to their demands? Some of each?

Color the map of Transylvania at the end of this unit while you discuss your ruling options.

LITHUANIA and POLAND

☺ ☻ **EXPLORATION: Castles of Lithuania**
The first castles of Lithuania were wooden. None of them survive today, but many sites have been excavated where they once stood. The castle of Voruta, an important castle of the 1200's will be rebuilt in the coming years as a faithful reproduction.

The wooden castles were built on hills and then large earthen berms, reinforced with horizontally placed logs were built. On top of this, wooden walls were built of whole logs, much like the frontier forts of North America of a much later period. Some of the walls would be a double thickness with room for men to stand inside on two levels. Built along the wall were towers for soldiers to stand in as lookouts and for archers to shoot from. Along the inside of the wall rooms were built: barracks for soldiers, blacksmith shops, stables, and so on. Inside the wall there would be other log buildings, a keep for the duke and his family and

---

Fabulous Fact

"Seats", as in "Saxon Seats" is an administrative term like district, province, or county.

Fabulous Fact

Modern Romania is formed of the countries of Transylvania, Wallachia, and Moldavia. The western half of this area was under the rule of the Hungarians through most of the middle ages, though most of the people were ethnically Romanian and not Hungarian. Modern Romania was formed after WWI as part of the treaty process.

Additional Layer

The word castle comes from the Latin word *castellum* which means fortified place. We think of castles as huge stone structures surrounded by moats, but early castles were more varied.

Wooden castles could be burned down, so eventually stone castles took their place. Stone castles were popular until artillery became strong enough to break through their walls. There isn't a building strong enough to withstand our current firepower.

Additional Layer
This map shows the Hanseatic League, a series of cities with trade treaties.

Colored areas are under the treaties, cities involved in the Hanseatic trading are shown as dots.

Additional Layer

This map shows the Grand Duchy of Lithuania to the east and the Kingdom of Poland to the west in about 1400 AD. Right now the two nations are at war, but in a little less than a hundred years they will unite by treaty against the common enemy of the Teutonic Knights. A few decades later they will unite and become one kingdom.

On the Web
http://youtu.be/Quld595ov6w
Short history of Poland.

perhaps other important buildings.

Build a model Lithuanian Castle from wood. You can use Lincoln Logs or craft sticks. Build it on a paper plate with a thick play dough base. We used hot glue to attach the cross pieces.

To make play dough:
½ c. salt
2 c. flour, mix well
Add 1 ½ cups boiling water, stir.
Add more flour until you have a non-sticky smooth dough.

You can color the dough by adding food coloring at any point. A mixture of blue, red, and yellow gives you a brown color.

☺ ☺ ● EXPLORATION: Growth of Cities
Lithuania began as a group of tribal communities headed by chiefs. Later one chief gained ascendancy over the others and became the Chief of Chiefs. They renamed their leaders Dukes and the Grand Duke. Through this time they were still an agricultural people with each duke owning a large tract of land and many private farmers owning their own land within the dukedom. Then in the 13th century, the town of Magdeburg in Germany had a brilliant idea. They would grant special privileges to people who settled and traded in their town because the trade would bring power and riches to the kingdom and the town. The special set of laws were called Magdeburg Rights. It worked. The town grew and became wealthy and powerful. Other towns all through eastern Europe began to adopt these laws and Lithuania and Poland were among them. This was the real beginning of

large towns in this area. The people in the towns had more freedoms and protected trade. The towns flourished. The cities in this region became part of a trade organization called the Hanseatic League.

Make a "help wanted" advertisement. You are a merchant who wants to trade with a town on the Baltic Coast, but you need people to help you: another merchant or two to travel with, a body of armed guards, a boy to help with the pack animals, and so on. Plan your trip, decide which goods you'll carry, and whether you'll go yourself or send a trusted employee. Watch out for bandits along the way.

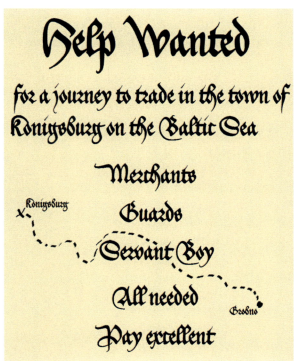

Write a description of your plans, a map of your route and dangers on your path. Don't forget the written instructions for your agent with your seal on it. Oh, the bothers of money!!!

☺ ◉ EXPLORATION: Lithuanian Religion
Lithuanians were a pagan people believing in a pantheon of gods until in 1385 King Wladyslaw II converted to Christianity and it became the cool thing among the nobility. The peasants held on to their old beliefs for generations more, slowly converting as well.

A Creation story: *In the beginning there was nothing but water, and Deivers (God) walked on the water. As he was rubbing two stones together he created a devil whose name was Liucius. Deivers commanded Liucius to dive down into the water and bring up soil and clay from the bottom. Liucius did this but also put some clay into his mouth. He gave the clay to Deivers who took it and spread it evenly upon the earth forming smooth land. Then Liucius, no longer able to keep the clay in his mouth, spit it out and this formed uneven, rocky and mountainous lands. Deivers laid down to sleep and Liucius tried to drag him into the*

Additional Layer

If Poland-Lithuania was so strong, how is it they were overrun during World War I and again in World War II?

By the time the 18th century came around Poland-Lithuania had weakened, partly because of their only semi-functional legislature. In 1772 Russia, Prussia, and Austria all invaded and seized land in Poland.

They signed a treaty between them, dividing the land up. Poland would be partitioned twice more, in 1793 and 1795. Poland would cease to exist as a nation until after World War I. Poland remained weak and was an easy target for Hitler's invasion of WWII.

Additional Layer

Technically, "pagan" means a belief system outside of the major religions – Christianity, Islam, and Judaism. For many people it has negative connotations beyond this simple definition though.

Additional Layer

Compare this creation story with the creation story in the Bible. Can you see similarities? Differences?

When you study mythology from all over the world you can often find many parallel stories. For example, there are many worldwide flood stories. Why do you think that so many cultures who had little or no contact with each other share similar stories?

Additional Layer

Jadwiga and Mary I of Hungary were sisters. Jadwiga was born a Hungarian, but as a child she was made heir of her childless uncle, the King of Poland. Both powerful ruling queens were of the Capetian House of Anjou, which makes them related to the kings of Hungary, Sicily, Naples, Poland and more distantly, France.

Additional Layer

Jadwiga was officially known as the King of Poland because she was a reigning monarch and not merely a consort.

Jadwiga is equivalent to the English name Hedwig.

water to drown him, but the land kept expanding under Deivers so he could not be drowned. Next both Deivers and Liucius competed to create animals. Deivers created good and useful animals like horses, dogs, sheep, birds, and cattle. Liucius created harmful creatures like snakes, mosquitoes, vultures and rats. So the good in the world comes from the God-Father, Deivers, and the evil in the world comes from the devil, Liucius.

Make this story into a booklet. In your own words, write the story throughout the pages, then illustrate it.

😊 🌐 EXPLORATION: A Child Bride

Princess Jadwiga of Poland was just ten years old when she became queen. In 1385 when she was twelve she was married off to Grand Duke Jogaila of Lithuania. This united the two kingdoms through treaty. But before she would marry Jogaila he had to become a Christian. He was baptized and took the name Wladyslaw, becoming King Wladyslaw II. Jadwiga continued to rule Poland as an independent sovereign until her death in 1399.

But before Jadwiga married Jogaila there was drama. Jadwiga, already a strong-willed young woman who knew her mind, wanted to marry William Hapsburg, Prince of Austria. Her advisers secretly conspired for her to wed the Pagan Grand Duke Jogaila. They wanted Polish prisoners freed, and a treaty between the two nations to fend off those rapacious Teutons in the north. William arrived at Krakow secretly and held secret meetings with the young queen. They planned a rendezvous, an escape, and a secret wedding. As Jadwiga fled the castle one night, axing her way out of a locked door, her father's trusted treasurer, an old man, begged her to do what was best for Poland rather than think of herself. She relented, stayed to marry the stranger Jogaila, and never saw William again.

Make puppets of the main characters of the story and put on a show. There are figures at the end of this unit or you can create your own. See the coloring sheet from the printables too.

🙂 🙂 EXPLORATION: How to Become a Serf

All people begin free. In Lithuania freedom was lost slowly over many generations. This is the most common way freedom is lost. Sometimes it happens quickly through war, but most often it is slow and insidious, step by step.

At first there were Dukes who administered large areas of land for the Grand Duke. On the lands were many free farmers who owned their own property and paid taxes to the Duke, who in turn paid taxes to the Grand Duke. In return the Grand Duke and Dukes protected the land from foreign invasion and criminals within. There were slaves, captured in war, who helped the farmers till their land. There were also some people who worked for the farmers as peasants, but these people were free and might hope one day to better their lot. After the Teutons began to destroy Prussia in the north, Prussian refugees who were peasants worked the land on the farms.

The Crusades changed all that. During the Crusades the pagan people of Lithuania were relentlessly attacked by the Teuton Knights. The Lithuanians could no longer rely on farmers and a few guards from the dukedoms to defend the kingdom. A class of warriors sprang up. They were called Boyars and they had nothing to do but train for war and fight.

The Boyars were given land as rewards for their service. But for the Duke to give land, first he had to take it from the free farm

Additional Layer

The Commonwealth of Poland and Lithuania, after 1569, had many aspects of a republic. The king was truly elected. The king was constrained by the legislature (Sejem) and the nobles, who controlled the Sejem. The people had religious freedom, the Sejem could veto laws of the king, including taxation, and astonishingly, they had the right to form an insurrection against the king if he broke the law. One of the bonuses for the people was that the Sejem generally vetoed war, allowing Poland to prosper when the rest of Europe was torn apart by the thirty years war. The height of the Polish Republic is called the Golden Liberty. Read more about what worked and didn't work in this experiment with freedom.

Writer's Workshop

If a poor man's daughter is going to die without medicine that the man can't afford, what would be the moral choice – steal the medicine and let her live, or don't steal it and be responsible for her death? Write your thoughts, and relate it to morals and law.

holders. This turned the farm holders into peasants as well. They no longer owned property and they were subject to the Boyars.

At first it probably seemed like a minor change. They no longer owned the land, but they still worked it and they still lived in their homes and they still had enough to eat and taxes were only a little higher than they had been before. Over time though, more and more of the rights of the peasants were eroded until the Boyars became absolute rulers over the lives and deaths of their people. The people had descended from free landholders with property and rights to serfdom. It took several generations, but it happened.

Do one of these:
1. Write a paragraph explaining how the free landholders became serfs.
2. Make a diagram showing the social structure before and after the Boyars gained control.

SERBIA

😃 😃 EXPLORATION: A New Law Code

In 1217 Serbia finally became a united and officially recognized kingdom. In 1219 they received permission to have their Christian church separate and independent from the church at Constantinople. At the same time, since they were independent, they needed to organize the kingdom, the church, and the law code to govern themselves. A priest named Sava, who also happened to be the king's brother, wrote a document called the Zakonopravilo. It is the Serbian Constitution based on Roman Law and Christianity and the Bible. Its use was transported throughout eastern Europe and it became the law code for Russia, Bulgaria, and Romania as well.

Sava

If you were going to write a whole new law code and organize a kingdom how would you do it? Not an easy question. People usually base their laws upon something that came before. What do you think the law code of your country is based on? Why? Do you see any relationship between morals and law? Who dictates what is moral? Discuss these ideas.

☻ ☻ EXPLORATION: Battle of Maritsa

The most powerful family of rulers in Serbian history were the Nemanjiks. They ruled from 1168 until 1371. Their first ruler was a charismatic man named Stefan who united the Serbs into one nation. All the rulers of this house took the name Stefan upon their ascending the throne as a title and mark of honor to their great ancestor. The last of the house was named Uros the Weak. He was called weak for good reason. He allowed his vassal lords to gain too much power, which divided the kingdom. When the Turks attacked, the kingdom couldn't withstand them for long.

One decisive defeat for the Serbs happened at the Battle of Maritsa in 1371. The Serbs were very sure of victory and began to celebrate a bit early, the night before the battle in fact. As they were lying drunk in their tents near the river Maritsa, the Ottomans came upon them in the dark and drove the Serbs into the river, killing and drowning many. The Serbs beat the Turks years later at the battle of Kosovo, holding the Turks back for awhile, but Serbia was weakened and fell eventually to the Turks in 1459. Their occupation lasted until 1804.

The battle plan for Maritsa was obviously not a good one on the part of the Serbs. Draw a map and design a better battle plan. How would you deploy your troops? What would you expect from your commanders and men? Include the river. You have 70,000 men. Your enemy has about ¼ of that number. Look up the Maritsa River in an atlas or online to see where it lies. The village that was nearby was called Chernomen. Today it is called Ormenio and is located in Greece.

☻ ☻ ☻ EXPLORATION: Serbian Monasteries

Unlike western Europe, many Serbians were literate. The monks of the independent Serbian Church taught literacy and learning to

A Serbian Monastery, shared under CC license by Lumen Roma

Additional Layer

Stefan Nemanja accepted Western Christianity and was able to have himself crowned king of Serbia by the Pope. Before this Serbia was a principality with a duke, but not raised to a kingdom. The Pope's crowning gave Serbia equality with other European Kingdoms. The same thing happened in other European countries as well. Why did a king require the pope's confirmation? Is there a modern standard that makes a nation or a ruler legitimate? What do you think of this concept, that you're not really a nation until we say you are? Pros and Cons?

Fabulous Fact

Gracanica Monastery was founded by King Stefan Milutin of Serbia in 1321.

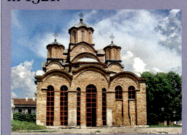
Photo by Laurent Drouet and shared under CC license on Wikimedia.

In 1984 the New Gracanica Monastery was built near Chicago, IL. It is a replica of the original building, but larger.

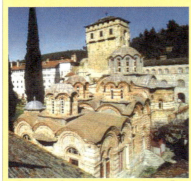
Fabulous Fact

Bulgaria became a nation in 681 when they separated from the Byzantines by treaty. From 1393 the Ottomans began a war of conquest, gaining more and more Bulgarian land.

Fabulous Fact

Bulgaria suffered under Ottoman rule. The people were taxed heavily, freedoms were curtailed, their culture was suppressed, and every fifth son was taken by the Sultan to undergo harsh training as a Janissary. People were not forced to become Muslim under the Ottomans, but life was much easier for them if they did.

many people so the people would understand Christianity and be able to read the Bible for themselves. The Church in the East used the common language of the people, wherever they lived. Look for images of Serbian illuminated texts and Serbian monasteries online to see what they were like. The manuscripts were written with the Cyrillic Alphabet, which was developed by a Byzantine monk early in the Middle Ages and is used through much of Eastern Europe.

BULGARIA

🙂 🙂 🙂 EXPLORATION: The Thracian Plain

When the Romans ruled the Mediterranean region there was a frontier of the empire in the northeast called Thrace. They were a barbarian, pagan people of tribesmen. Later, when western Rome fell, the area remained under eastern Roman (or Byzantine) control. But waves of Barbarians from north and east began to overrun the Thracians. Some of these were the Slavs from the north and the Bulgars from the east. They settled on the Thracian Plain and the Sofia Basin, won independence from the Byzantines, and set up a stable pagan feudal monarchy. This was the beginnings of Bulgaria.

Why fight over the Thracian Plain? What made it so desirable? Natural resources and strategic locations often make areas desirable. Are there any areas in the United States that are more desirable than others? What makes them so?

A view of the upper Thracian Plain and the city of Silven, shared under CC license by Evgeni Dinev.

Make of model of the Thracian plain and Sofia Basin from salt dough. After it has dried, paint it. Include rivers, mountains, and cities that were there in the Middle Ages.

This map shows the region the Romans called Thrace.

😊 😊 😊 **EXPLORATION: King of Bulgaria**

Make a character sketch of one of these Bulgarian rulers of the Middle Ages:

- Asparukh
- Kroum
- Boris I
- Simeon I
- Samuel
- Kaloyan
- Ivan Asen II

Draw or print out a picture of the person and put it in the center of the page, then scatter several facts about them around their picture. You can develop it into a complete biography if you like.

This is Boris I of Bulgaria

Famous Folks

Petar Delyan was the leader of a Bulgarian uprising that threw off Ottoman rule. He became the first king of Bulgaria in 1041.

He only lasted one year though. One night when he was drunk, his cousin, Alusian, treacherous son of a treacherous father, cut off Delyan's nose and blinded him with a kitchen knife. Delyan wasn't dead, but his cousin took the throne, soon after fleeing to the enemy, the Byzantines.

In spite of his blindness, Delyan took back command of the troops in the rebellion. Delyan perished in battle. Some legends say at the hand of Harald Hardrada, future king of Norway, and the invader who attacked the English King Harold at Stamford Bridge, weakening him for the later invasion of William of Normandy. Hardrada was in Byzantium at the time fighting as a mercenary in the Varangian troops.

GEOGRAPHY: HUNGARY

On the Web

So what happened in 1956 in Hungary? Revolt against the Soviets. Watch the BBC special here:

http://youtu.be/iU3xY-h_uGk

Here is what communism really looks like.

Teaching Tip

We often recommend fairy tales in the library lists when doing country studies. Fairy tales, if read intelligently, give a window into the attitudes and the worldview of a people. You can see what they value. Does the hero win though hard work, through cunning, with the help of others, or by himself? What are the attitudes about government or power? What animals or people or objects are magical? Are they everyday sorts of things you might find in any home or are they remote and mystical? People tell stories for a reason and that reason is usually to pass on values and belief systems. So if you want to understand another culture and what is at their core, read their stories.

Up until the end of World War I and the reparations that followed, Hungary was a great and powerful empire in Europe. The treaties of 1918 reduced the territory by about 70%. Besides that, Hungary lost all its ports and was forced to pay war reparations. From then until the present, Hungary has been ruled by one authoritarian regime after another.

The Danube River flows through Budapest. Across the river you see the buildings of Parliament. Photo by Heinz Albers, CC license.

In 1956 Hungary rebelled against communist Russian rule. The rebellion was put down forcibly and violently, and the Prime Minister of Hungary was executed. Thousands of Hungarians fled to America and other places. The borders with Austria finally opened up in 1989, aiding in the fall of the eastern bloc. Hungary repealed many of the laws governing economics allowing for more and more free market practices. They also set up a parliamentary republic and held free elections. They are still a heavily socialist welfare state. Hungary has one of the highest standards of living for eastern Europe and is a tourist destination for many people.

Hungary lies in the center of the Carpathian Basin, also known as the Pannonian Basin. The country is rimmed by mountain ranges around this fertile plain. Rivers run through the country, providing water for farming and industry. The Danube runs north to south, nearly dividing the country in two. The climate is continental with hot summers and cold winters. They have snowfall every winter.

☺ ☺ ☺ EXPLORATION: Color a map of Hungary
Include the major cities and rivers and other landscape features. You can find a blank outline map at the end of this unit. Use a student atlas to fill in the details.

It can be fun to find out some facts or landmarks about the country and place them around the map on a poster board. Draw a line to point out the location on the map.

☺ ☺ EXPLORATION: Nature Scene of Hungary
You need paint, card stock, and glue.

1. Research what the Hungary landscape is like. Paint a picture on card stock to look like the landscape.

Famous Folks

Albert Szent-Györgyi discovered Vitamin C and made the first synthetic vitamins, forever ending the threat of scurvy and winning the Nobel Prize.

Fabulous Fact

The Rubik's Cube was invented by a Hungarian named Ernő Rubik.

Fabulous Fact

Hungary is an exceedingly beautiful land with many peaceful landscapes like this one.

There is a long distance walking path (we would call it a hiking trail in the U.S.) that crosses the Hungarian countryside for more than 1,000 kilometers. Along the way you see beautiful and breathtaking natural wonders, lakes, mountains, green rolling fields, dozens of picturesque castles, churches, palaces, and windmills. It is called the Countrywide Blue Tour. Walk a portion of it if you ever go to Hungary.

This church is 900 years old.

2. Carefully cut windows in the card stock picture in various places, leaving one side attached as a flap.
3. Draw or paint small pictures of animals native to Hungary to go inside each of the windows. (you can also cut pictures from a magazine or print them from the Internet.)
4. Glue the animal pictures onto colored card stock and glue each animal picture into a window of your landscape painting.
5. After it's all dry, you can write the name of each animal inside the flap of the window.

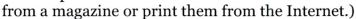

☺ ☺ ☺ EXPLORATION: Goulash

Hungarians eat spicy food, especially when compared to the rest of Europe. Their favorite spice is hot paprika, which they invented. They also eat meat, seasonal vegetables, and delicate tasty pastries.

Goulash Stew
1 pound cubed stew meat
1 tsp. salt
¼ tsp. pepper
4 cups chopped onion
2 cloves garlic
2 Tbsp. paprika (reduce amount if your family isn't used to hot things.)
1 Tbsp. red wine vinegar
1 cup chopped tomato
2 bay leaves
1½ cups water
1 cup beef broth
2 ½ cups peeled potatoes

Saute meat, salt, pepper, onion, and garlic in small amount of oil until browned. Add remaining ingredients and bring to a boil. Cover and simmer for an hour. Watch the liquid level and add more water as needed.

You can serve it as a stew or over cooked egg noodles.

☺ ☺ ☺ **EXPLORATION: Music**
The most famous Hungarian pianist
and composer is Franz Liszt. Listen
to some of his music. You can also
listen and view Hungarian folk music
on You Tube. Your library also
should have some CD's from
Hungary.

☺ ☺ **EXPLORATION: Facts**
Make a fact sheet for Hungary.
Include information on languages,
religions, ethnic groups, population,
type of government and so on. Draw
a picture of the flag on the sheet as
well. You can find the information in a student atlas or online.

☺ ☺ **EXPLORATION: Names**
In Hungary the family name comes first, followed by the given
name. For example in the next exploration we'll learn about
Miklos Toldi. But in Hungary they would call him Toldi Miklos.
Toldi is the family name and Miklos is his given name.

Women in Hungary used to take their husband's whole name
when marrying and add the suffix -ne, which means Mrs. So if
Toldi had a wife her name would be Toldine Miklos. But these
days women usually keep their given names, only adopting their
husband's family name and adding the -ne suffix to the family
name.

If you have a traditional English name you may be able to find its
equivalent in Hungarian. Here are a few. You can find your
name by searching for "Equivalent English names in Hungarian"
on the Internet.

Michelle/ Michael = Miska	Nicholas = Miklos
Melissa = Melita	Aaron = Aron
Alexander/ Alexis = Sander	Andrew = Andor
Issac = Izsak	Jacob = Jakab
Sarah = Sarika	Timothy = Timot
Elisabeth = Izabella	Rachel = Rahel

☺ ☺ ☺ **EXPLORATION: A National Hero**
Every nation has its heroes it looks up to. In America we have the
Pilgrims, Founding Fathers, the astronauts of the space age and
so on. One of Hungary's heroes is Miklos Toldi. He was a knight
of exceptional strength and skill. He rose from the lower ranks to

Additional Layer
Hungary is home to the
world's largest thermal
cave system. Learn how
thermal caves are
formed.

Additional Layer

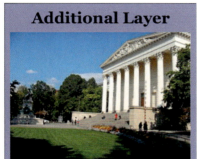

Uh, oh, there are the
Greeks again. This is the
Hungarian National
Museum building.

This is the Budapest Art
Museum done in an art
deco style.

Hungary is full of
gorgeous architecture.

On the Web
We love this video
featuring the Hungarian
landscape and
Hungarian folk music.
http://youtu.be/G7JNKu
ProrM
And here's a 1936 clip:
http://youtu.be/ggFHQC
KF2HY

On the Web

Hungarian folk dance called Urgos, or "Jumping Dance":

http://youtu.be/213e0w NkVlw

Additional Layer

In Hungary instead of celebrating your birthday, you would celebrate your name day. This is the day that is set apart in the Roman Catholic calendar for your saint. You might get flowers or gifts on that day.

Writer's Workshop

We definitely have national heroes, but chances are you have some personal heroes too if you stop and think about it.

A hero is someone who has qualities we admire and would like to possess. We are usually better people from having known them or known of their lives, characteristics, or achievements.

Choose one of your personal heroes and write about that person. What makes your hero heroic to you? What qualities do you admire? How have you become better because of him or her?

become the king's own knight and rule over counties of his own. He's so famous that modern Hungarian army tanks are called Toldis after him.

Teens and adults may enjoy reading the epic poem by Janos Arany, *Toldi*. Just be careful you're buying it in an English translation. Or you can read it online here: http://mek.niif.hu/00500/00595/html/epics2.htm. It's not too long and though it's told poetically, it is a riveting tale with lots of heroism and fights.

Younger kids will enjoy drawing a picture of what they think Miklos Toldi looks like after they hear this introduction of him from the poem *Toldi* by Arany:

Like a herdsman's fire blazing on autumn nights across the vast sea of the puszta, the face of Miklós Toldi flares before me over nine or ten generations of antique time. I see, it seems, his towering form and the thrust of his lance in scorching battle. The thundering sound of his voice I hear you would now conceive as the wrath of God.

This was the man, when needed, who stood his ground. There is no one to match him now in the seven parts of the realm. If he were to rise up and walk among you, his works would appear a sorcery. Three of you would never withstand the weight of his club, his sling or spear. Your blood would run cold at his terrible shield and the spurs he wore upon his boots.

☺ ☻ EXPLORATION: Horse Nation

Hungarians have been breeding and riding and loving horses for at least a thousand years. Use the Hungarian Horses Printable from the end of this unit. Color the horse any way you like. Cut out the horse and semi circle. Fold a paper plate in half and glue the horse to the plate so the horse sticks out above the flat folded edge. Now your horse can rock back and forth. Read the facts about Hungarian horses.

On the craft, the text reads: **Hungarian** / **Horse**

Bred from a mix of Arabian, Turkic, Mongolian, and Iberian horses

Bred for strength and endurance

Military horses and farm horses

The Hungarian government used to have farms where they bred horses, mostly for the military

Nonius, Kisber Felver, and Hungarian Warmblood are three different breeds of Hungarian horse

Csikos are the men who herd horses on the puszta, the Hungarian cattle country

Mezohegyes is a town, the home of the state horse breeding program

The Nonius breed of horses is still used for agriculture

(No, the horse in the craft is just a generic horse, not specifically a Hungarian horse—just in case you're a horse lover.)

😊 🌍 EXPLORATION: Hungarian Hopscotch
Hungarian hopscotch is played like American hopscotch, except with an extra twist. You throw your stone out on a square, begin to hop, but then when you come to the square with the stone you must balance the stone on your head through the rest of the game. Hop carefully, because you lose if you fail to balance the stone!

😊 🌍 EXPLORATION: Walking Around The Castle
To play this Hungarian game a group of kids needs to stand in a circle. Then you sing this song to play:

Chain, chain, turning chain
Chain, chain, turning chain
Chain, chain, turning chain
Tyler should turn outward
Tyler's chain!

*(fill in various children's names from the circle)

Then Tyler would lead the circle out and around "the castle" (the circle of kids), eventually reversing the direction of the circle. Then you begin the song again, with Tyler calling out a new child's name to be the leader the next time because he was the last leader.

On the Web
Learn to draw a horse by yourself.

There are many how-to-draw tutorials. Here is one:
http://www.howtodrawanimals.net/how-to-draw-a-horse

On the Web
Wowzers! Watch this Hungarian man gallop on the backs of five horses.
http://youtu.be/qbYTJFZ36EQ

Then watch this short video of a tour of Hungarian cowboy country, the Puszta.
http://youtu.be/oDRZdvU-7S8

More Crafts
Whole bunches of fun Hungarian themed crafts: http://www.dltk-kids.com/world/hungary/

Besides having to balance the hopscotch rock, some Hungarian versions of the game also set the board up in a snail shape. The kids start on the biggest squares on the outside, and then progressively the squares get smaller and smaller as you spiral inward on the snail.

Additional Layer

Besides Christmas and Easter, here are the other important holidays of Hungary:

<u>New Year's Day</u>
In Hungary New Year's Day is celebrated with eating lentil soup and pork, visiting family and friends and wishing everyone a Happy New Year.

<u>March 15th</u>
This commemorates the revolution of 1848.

<u>May 1st</u>
European Labor Day.

<u>Whit Monday</u>
The Monday following Whitsun or Pentecost is a Christian feast, celebrating the descent of the Holy Spirit.

<u>August 20th</u>
St. Stephen's Day is the great national holiday that celebrates the foundation of Hungary. It's like Hungary's 4th of July with parties and fireworks in the evening.

<u>October 23rd</u>
October 23rd commemorates the revolution of 1956, Hungary's uprising against communism.

<u>November 1st</u>
'All Saint's Day' is a traditional day of honoring the memory of the deceased. It's a custom to light candles and visit the graves of passed relatives.

There are no winners or losers. It's just fun for all, kind of like our own Ring Around the Rosie.

☺ ☻ ☻ **EXPLORATION: Happy Easter Hungary**

In Hungary Easter is an important spring holiday. It usually coincides with their spring festival, which is a two week long event full of parades, parties, concerts, and other celebrations. They also decorate eggs in a big way! The eggs aren't all this large, but they are this ornate. Their eggs aren't solid colors; they have colorful swirls, floral prints, and designs.

Hungarian Easter Egg, shared under CC license by J. Donahoe

They often use batik techniques, but you can use a simpler method. Imitate their style on clean, dry, hard boiled eggs using fine point permanent markers. The metallic markers give a fascinating appearance. Draw your own design on the egg with the permanent markers. You can add flowers, stripes, polka dots – any design you like. Don't eat the eggs right away. Just enjoy the design for a bit.

☺ ☻ **EXPLORATION: Hungarian Christmas**
Christmas is a very family-centered holiday in Hungary. The people don't go to parties, they stay home and celebrate Christmas Eve and Christmas Day with their loved ones. They

don't have outdoor decorations, but they do decorate inside their homes. Christmas trees aren't decorated earlier in the month as we do in the United States. Instead, the children believe that angels bring the decorated trees on Christmas Eve. When the tree bell rings, the children rush in to see the tree. Presents surround the Christmas tree. On Christmas Day the family has a big dinner, usually fish and cabbage, and then they open gifts.

Use the angel worksheet at the end of this unit to make your own decorated Christmas tree.

☺ ☺ ☻ EXPLORATION: Budapest
Go to You Tube for a little tour of some of the sites of Budapest, the capital city of Hungary. There are quite a few excellent videos to check out. Here's a cool, speed motion one:
http://youtu.be/lfz4T5cPaQs

When you are finished reading and viewing the sites fo the city make a travel plan about the top five places in Budapest you will see if you go there. Include a picture from the Internet and some facts about each site.

☺ ☻ EXPLORATION: Hungarian Dogs
There are several breeds of dog that are native to Hungary. You can read a little about them on this site:
http://www.hungarotips.com/customs/kutyak.html

This dog to the right is a Hungarian Komondor.

Choose one of the breeds, look up more information and make a paper bag puppet to look like the breed you've chosen. Write a short report, glue it to the back of the paper bag puppet and present your information to an audience.

☺ ☺ ☻ EXPLORATION: Hungarian Tales
Visit this website to read some traditional Hungarian fairy tales:
http://www.mainlesson.com/display.php?author=orczy&book=hungarian&story=_contents
See if you can identify some values of the people of Hungary.

SCIENCE: METALS

Memorization Station

We included a black and white Periodic Table of the Elements at the end of this unit. Have your kids color in the different groups of metals and memorize characteristics of each group.

Definition

An alloy is a mixture of two or more elements, at least one of them being a metal.

Metals are mixed with each other and with non-metals to give certain properties, like increased strength, greater ductility, or reduced conductivity.

Additional Layer

Metals form into crystals just like other elements.

Here are some gallium crystals.

Metals are elements where the electrons are arranged in rows. The electrons are easily removed and can move from atom to atom easily. This allows electricity to conduct easily. Remember that electricity is just flowing electrons.

Metals have some characteristics more or less in common. Most of them conduct electricity, are malleable (easy to pound into shapes), are ductile (can be pulled into a wire), have a high boiling point, are hard, and have a shiny grayish color. But not all metals have all those characteristics. Gold is yellow, not silver. Mercury is liquid at room temperature, and sodium is very soft.

There are different major classes of metals: alkali metals, alkaline earth metals, transition metals, poor metals, and semi-metals. Which type they are depends on their characteristics, which depends on the numbers of protons and neutrons and electrons they have. You can see these categories on a periodic table clearly.

Alkali metals are in group 1 (the far left column) on the periodic table. They react with water easily to form alkaline (basic) solutions. The alkali metals are all silvery-white in color and are extremely reactive. In their pure form they corrode within minutes in air contact and must be stored in oil to prevent this. Some of them include sodium, lithium, and potassium. Because of their reactivity they are not found in their pure state in nature very often.

Periodic Table of the Elements

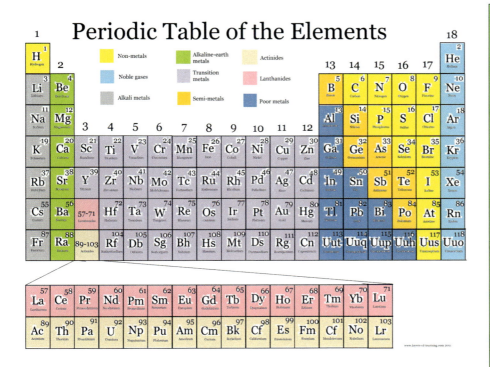

Additional Layer

Sometime in the 14th century in Japan at least one unknown sword maker sprinkled his steel with traces of Molybdenum, a very hard metal with an extremely high melting point. This alloy made incredibly tough swords.

The technology was lost though and not rediscovered until the Germans used it in the plating of their tanks during WWI.

Alkaline earth metals are in period 2 of the periodic table. They include calcium, beryllium, and magnesium. They also react with water to form alkali solutions. The name "earth" is in their name because they are commonly found in nature in compound forms. They are not quite as reactive as the alkali metals but they behave similarly and have similar properties.

Transition metals are in periods 3 through 10 on the periodic table including the two bottom rows that are set apart on the table. Iron, nickle, silver, platinum, and gold are all transition metals, plus many more that you are probably less familiar with. They are all shiny, hard, and have high melting points. These metals are very similar to their neighbors in the periodic table. These metals are much less reactive than the alkali and alkaline earth metals, but they do conduct electricity well for the most part.

The poor metals are called this because they are softer and weaker than the other metals. They are still very useful though. They include lead, aluminum, and tin. They are used most often in alloys. These metals are found in periods 13 through 16 of the periodic table, but they do not include the whole period (see the chart above).

The semi-metals are found in periods 13 through 16 as well. They are called semi-metals because they have properties

Writer's Workshop

Imagine you just found a gold mine on your property. What would you do next? Who would you tell?

Write a story about what you might do.

Additional Layer

There is a special category of metals known as noble metals. Like the noble gases, the Noble Metals don't react easily. Therefore, they can be found in a pure form in nature. Gold, silver, copper, palladium, and platinum are the noble metals. Check your periodic table to see where they are located.

Gold nugget, courtesy USGS

Memorization Station

Memorize the properties of metals:

    conductivity

    malleability

    luster

Many metals are also ductile.

Additional Layer

Fireworks use metals both for burning and for the colors and light they produce. Learn more about fireworks.

like the metals, but also have properties like non-metals. They may look like metals, but not conduct electricity for example. They combine well with metals to make alloys. Some of them include silicone, boron, and arsenic.

☺ ☻ EXPERIMENT: Burning Metal

You need steel wool and a 9V battery.

1. Pull the steel wool apart to enlarge it and make more air spaces.
2. Place it in a metal pan or outside on concrete, somewhere it will be safe to start a small fire.
3. Touch the battery to the steel wool and hold it there until it catches fire.

The steel wool starts on fire because the iron filings are surrounded by more air than there would be if the iron were densely packed in a solid bar.

☻ EXPERIMENT: Flame Testing

Different chemicals burn with different colors. You can use the color of the flame given off to test for which type of metal you have. This an experiment to be performed by an adult with the kids observing or by a teen with adult supervision. Everyone should wear safety glasses and the experiment performer should wear protective gloves.

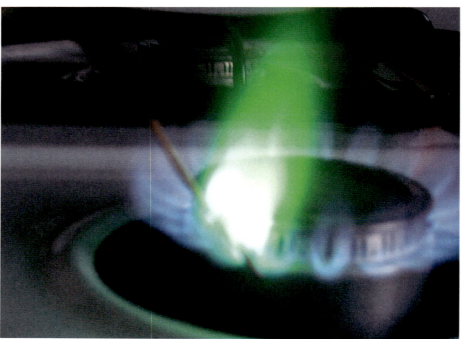

Copper flame test

1. Obtain wire from the hardware store in several different types of metals. You can use lead solder, perfectly safe to handle as long as you don't eat it. There are also different types of metal wire available at craft stores in the jewelry making department.
2. Hold the wire in a Bunsen burner flame or flame from a butane torch. A candle or match flame is not hot enough. You can buy a butane lab burner from Home Science Tools online or another science supply store for about $50. If you have a gas stove, the flame from the burner works too.
3. Hold one wire sample at a time in the flame until it heats enough to begin burning on its own.
4. Observe the colors of the flame coming from each sample.

Metals give off different colors because when the atoms are excited by the heat they give off light. The same principle is responsible for the colors of fireworks and the colors of the northern lights. Some metals do not change the color of the flame. Also if sodium impurities are present, a common problem, the flame will look orange no matter what else is present.

Lead = blue   Copper = blue-green
Sodium = orange   Barium = brown-green
Potassium = lilac   Lithium = red
Aluminum =bright, silver   Iron = gold
Zinc = bluish-green

😊 😊 😊 EXPERIMENT: More Fun With Fire

You can prep pine cones to burn with colored flame. Soak each pine cone in alcohol mixed with a single colorant. Or you can mix the colorant with water, then allow the pine cones to completely dry before you try to burn them. Each of the colorants below can be purchased in nearby stores and each has a different metal as its main ingredient.

- Calcium Chloride – laundry supply, bleaching agent
- Sodium Chloride – Table salt
- Borax – Laundry
- Copper Sulfate – Swimming pool supplies
- Potassium chloride – Salt substitute, found in grocery stores
- Magnesium sulfate – Epsom salts, drug store

Just get a campfire going and throw your specially prepared pine cones on to see what will happen. Record which colors you get with each chemical.

Additional Layer

These are countries in the world where gold mining takes place.

Additional Layer

Legend has it that a Chinese cook once accidentally spilled saltpeter into a cooking fire. An interesting flame was produced. Saltpeter was used as a flavoring salt, but it is more commonly an ingredient in gunpowder. Charcoal and sulfur were also common in early fires, and are other ingredients of gunpowder. The mixture burned with a pretty flame in a fire, and it exploded if it was enclosed in a bamboo tube. And that was the beginning of fireworks.

Additional Layer

A base metal is one that corrodes quickly and reacts easily with hydrochloric acid. Sometimes base metals are seen as the opposite of noble metals. Iron, nickle, lead, and zinc are base metals.

8cm

This is lead ore, the rock lead is extracted from. Photo courtesy USGS.

Alchemists considered any inexpensive common metal to be a base metal. The opposite would have been a precious metal like gold or silver.

Additional Layer

This is a diagram of the electron shells of lead.

82: Lead   2,8,18,32,18,4

Pb

It is a very large, very heavy atom, the largest stable atom in fact. Which is why it can shield radiation.

☺ ☻ EXPERIMENT: Conductivity

You need several spoons made of metal, plastic, and wood, and some hot water.

Place each of the spoons into hot water at the same time and see which one gets hot the fastest. The speed at which it heats is called its conductivity. Why do you think we use metal pans instead of wood? There is more than one reason.

☺ ☻ EXPERIMENT: Electrical conductivity

You need a D battery, wire, a light bulb, and some metal coins and other metal objects.

1. Set up a conduction apparatus with wire running from the D battery (you can tape it on) to a light bulb (touch one wire to the bottom of the light bulb and the other to the side of the base).
2. Place the opposite end of the battery and the base of the light bulb on the object to test for conductivity. Try some plastic, metal, glass, and other objects.
3. If the light bulb lights up you have found conductive materials.

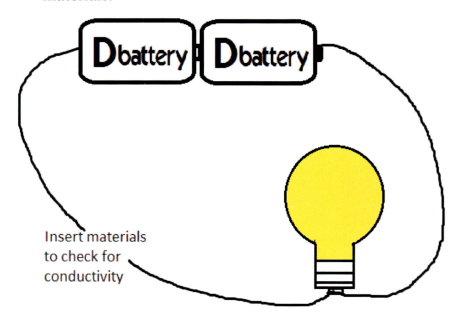

Insert materials to check for conductivity

☻ ☺ EXPERIMENT: Chemical Reactivity of Metals

You need vinegar, a container, and several different types of metal objects: iron nail, copper pennies, silver ring, gold earrings, aluminum foil, etc.

1. Pour about a cup of vinegar into a container, enough to cover the metal objects you will drop in.

2. Drop in metal objects
3. Observe which ones have bubbles form on them.

Bubble formation is an indication that a reaction is happening. The more bubbles, the stronger the reaction. Make a list from most reactive to least. Compare your list to where these metals appear on the periodic table.

(Note: the list may not turn out perfect since the metals you find around the house are all alloys and not pure, still it should be pretty good.)

☺ ☻ EXPLORATION: Reaction Power

Draw a diagram of a highly reactive potassium ion. Potassium and other alkali metals by themselves are extremely reactive. Why are some elements more reactive than others? Completed and fulfilled atoms always have 8 electrons in their outer shell, the outermost level of electrons. Alkali metals, like potassium and sodium, are so reactive because they have just one electron in their outer shell, the easiest way for them to become stable is to lose that one electron. Sounds like no big deal, right? Forces on the atomic scale are, well, massive (think atom bombs for instance). When a pure alkali metal reacts with moisture, even just water vapor in the air, it usually explodes violently. In the experiment below the potassium is combined with nitrogen, which fulfills potassium's electron needs and so makes a stable compound, until you burn it anyway.

Here's a diagram of a Potassium atom, with that one electron in its outermost shell. Draw one of your own, labeling that reactive electron in the outer shell. Find potassium on the periodic table.

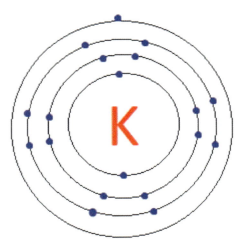

☺ ☺ ☻ EXPERIMENT: Smoke Bombs

This is a way cool experiment to wow the kids and neighbors. It really should be called smoke and fire bombs.

1. Mix 1/2 cup saltpeter (found at some drug stores, call around to see who has it) with 1/2 cup sugar in a saucepan.

On the Web
Steel is made of iron mixed with carbon and other elements, depending on the purpose intended. There are thousands of different "recipes".

Want to see the process?

http://youtu.be/9l7Jqon yoKA

Here's another, longer and older, video about the way iron is mined and then turned into steel.

http://youtu.be/YV9mM YUkERU

Additional Layer
We use steel constantly in our every day lives. Cars, cooking pans, watches, knives, power lines, industry, canned foods, and much more all use steel. Perhaps one of the most important uses of steel is in national defense. American steel production has been declining since the 1970's. See if you can discover the causes of the decline. Is it bad, good, or not important to the United States?

Additional Layer
Why is the chemical symbol for Potassium a "K"? Go find out.

Additional Layer

Find out about saltpeter, where does it come from? Who first invented it? What did they use it for? Why do drugstores today carry it?

Writer's Workshop

Learn about the history of matches. Who invented them? What's the difference between a "strike anywhere" and a "safety match"? What is smoke? Write your discoveries.

Additional Layer

Try pouring 1/2 cup of sugar into a cup by itself and lighting it on fire. What happens?

Additional Layer

South Africa is the world's leading producer of gold, diamonds, and platinum, which explains why the British were so interested.

Heat over medium to high heat, stirring constantly, until the sugar melts. You will have a stiff liquid.

2. Pour into a paper cup carefully. It's hot!
3. Let it cool for a bit, then stick several wooden matches down in the cooling sugar mixture, with the match heads up.
4. Let it cool completely.
5. Set your smoke bomb outside on a sidewalk or driveway, where it can't catch anything on fire. It's cool to do this at night or in the evening, when the light is low. Light the matches and the paper cup, then stand back. It will smolder for awhile and then take off, producing a spectacular flame and lots and lots of smoke.

Ah, chemistry at its finest.

The sugar, containing lots of carbon, burns fabulously. Burning is one form of oxidation, the process where positive charges are added to a chemical.

The saltpeter, Potassium nitrate, facilitates the burning and produces the solid, which rises into the air = smoke.
Here's the reaction:

potassium nitrate + sugar → nitrogen gas + potassium carbonate + carbon dioxide + water

Using chemical symbols:

$$KNO_3 + C_{12}H_22O_{11} \rightarrow N_2 + K_2CO_3 + CO_2 + H_2O$$

(Note that this chemical equation is not balanced according to moles in the reaction. If you don't know what that means, don't worry about it.)

😊 🙂 EXPERIMENT: Identify a Metal
Give your kids a metal object and have them use their knowledge of metals to identify it.

Some possibilities: gold or silver jewelry (high Karat content, 14K or higher), nail, wire, or aluminum. Be sure you know which metal it is and read up on the properties before you give it to them.

1. They should determine first if it is a metal. What is the definition? How can you test it?
2. Which kind of metal? How reactive is it? What color is it? What color is the flame when it is heated?
3. Narrow it down and then have them read about their guesses.
4. Are there any other tests they can use to be sure?
5. Write the hypothesis with their reasoning.

Reveal to them which metal you gave them and discuss the process they used to identify it.

Variation: Get four pieces of wire, each a different metal. Tell the kids which four metals they have, but not which is which. Have the kids determine which type of metal each wire is.

😊 🙂 EXPERIMENT: Glass
Silicon dioxide is one of the most common and cheap of all compounds on Earth. One of its main components is silicon, a semi-metal. Silicon dioxide is the main ingredient in glass production, electronic circuits, and is used in alloys of steel. We can't make real glass out of silicon, but we can make fake glass just for fun.

1. Line a baking sheet with wax paper and lightly spray the wax paper with cooking spray.
2. Place 1 cup sugar in a sauce pan.
3. Turn the heat to low.
4. Heat and stir constantly until the sugar melts completely.
5. Pour on to the prepared baking sheet.
6. Let cool, then you can peel off the wax paper and eat it!

Silicon is made into glass in the same basic way. The silicon sand is heated at extremely high temperatures until it melts together.

Additional Layer

Okay, if you need a refresher on balancing chemical equations watch this video from Khan Academy:

http://youtu.be/RnGu3x O2h74

Then balance the equations in this unit.

Additional Layer

Metallic looking paints actually have powdered metal in them to give them that luster and shine. You can make your own metallic paint: http://www.ehow.com/h ow_5709520_make-metallic-paint.html

Additional Layer

Silicon Valley got its name because that area near San Francisco, California, is a hub of electronics and computer chip production. There are quite a few other tech-heavy cities in the United States, but none as famous as Silicon Valley.

Photo by Samykolon and shared under CC license on Wikimedia.

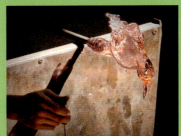
Traces of other elements are added to give strength or colors or other qualities to the glass, then the glass is poured or blown or turned into the shapes that are desired.

☺ ☻ ☻ EXPEDITION: Recycling Center
Metals are one of the most recycled of materials. See if you can take a tour of a local recycling plant. Ask them about the amount of energy and cost it takes to recycle materials versus the amount of energy and cost required to manufacture them from raw materials. Remember the amount of energy is closely related to the cost.

☺ ☻ ☻ EXPEDITION: Mining for Metals
Some mines, either operating or historic, have tours available to the public. See if you can arrange one if you live near enough. Before you go, learn more about the metals they are mining for in that location and the mining processes so you can ask intelligent questions of your guide.

If you don't live near a mining operation with tours, then take an armchair expedition to the Stillwater Paladium Mine of Montana. www.stillwaterpalladium.com.

☺ ☻ EXPERIMENT: Copper Plating
You can coat iron nails with copper with this simple experiment. You need nails, pennies, salt, vinegar, and a glass or plastic bowl.
1. Put 1 cup of vinegar into a bowl and a teaspoon of salt.
2. Add 10-15 copper pennies to the bowl. Let it sit for ten minutes. Fish the pennies out and lay them on a paper towel to dry.
3. Place an un-galvanized nail into the vinegar solution and let it sit for 30 minutes or more.

When your pennies come out of the vinegar solution they will be very bright and clean looking. The vinegar is an acid that has eaten away some of the metal on the pennies. As a result there is copper left in the vinegar solution. When you put the iron nail in the vinegar you should have noti9ced bubbles on the surface of the nail. This is evidence that a reaction is happening. A copper coating is left on the nail.

If you don't wash your pennies you will notice a green coating after a few hours. This is reaction between oxygen and copper taking place. The vinegar and salt acted as catalysts making the reaction happen much more quickly than it normally would.

THE ARTS: PRINTMAKING

Today we have rubber stamps, copy machines, scanners, and printers. It's easy to make multiples of things if we want to, but this was not always the case. Printmaking has served this purpose throughout most of history, but it's also become an art form of its very own.

Melencolia by Albrecht Dürer, a print made by engraving

The Sumerians needed to mark the things they owned, so they carved images into cylinders which they pressed into wet clay, essentially stamping it with their mark. The Chinese made rubbings from carved texts to make prints. They also invented paper, which made printmaking more possible on a grand scale than ever before. With paper, printmaking flourished. Artists

Additional Layer

Now we have the capability to scan and copy art digitally and with a copy machine, but technically those don't count as art prints. For example, the paintings we print in Layers of Learning units aren't fine art. They are just pictures of fine art, worth nothing on their own.

Additional Layer

For about as long as people have been making art, people have been forging art. Forgers try to create something just like the masters and pass it off as real pieces.

Famous Folks

Rembrandt's mastery of intaglio enabled him to create over three hundred printmaking plates.

could spread art and knowledge to huge numbers of people by printing. Woodcut prints were common, but then Gutenberg's movable type brought printmaking to a whole new level. The general population now had art and literature, not just royals, monks, and scholars.

Beginning with the Renaissance, printmaking techniques began to be an art. Woodcuts prints and engravings eventually expanded to include etching, silkscreen, linoleum prints, monoprint, mezzotint, and lithography. Print shops began to employ master printers, who collaborated with artists to create art. Now almost everything artists create is made in multiples and disseminated.

☺ ☺ ☺ EXPLORATION: Scratch Foam Prints
You need scratch foam or Styrofoam, scissors, a tool to press lines into the foam (Popsicle stick, pencil, etc.), printing ink, a rubber brayer, and paper.

1. Cut the basic shape you want out of your foam.
2. Etch lines into the foam with a tool like a Popsicle stick. You can just make a random design or you can create pictures. Whatever you choose, you may want to sketch out your plan first.
3. Roll ink over the foam with a rubber brayer and then press paper onto the foam stamp.

A fun variation on this is to first create a watercolor background for your scratch foam print.

☺ ☻ EXPLORATION: Biography

Do some research and write a biography about one of these famous printmakers:

- Turner
- Whistler
- Blake
- Degas
- Cassatt
- Goya
- Chagall
- Matisse
- Munch
- Picasso
- Miro
- Arp
- Ernst
- Dali
- Kandinsky
- Klee

☺ ☻ EXPLORATION: Yarn Printing

You need a piece of cardboard, glue, and yarn. Draw a design onto the cardboard, which should be the same size or a little smaller than your paper. Glue yarn over the lines in the design. Brush paint or printing ink over the yarn and then use as a stamp.

☺ ☻ EXPLORATION: Potato Stamps

Anything you can carve into can become a stamp. Woodcut prints were very popular early printing tools, but wood is a hard substance for kids to carve into. You can carve designs much more easily with something soft, like a potato.

There are four basic kinds of printmaking:

1. Relief printing is creating a print from a raised surface – rubber stamps and woodcuts are relief.

2. Intaglio prints are made by cutting into a surface and applying the ink into the grooves instead of on the raised surfaces. Etching is a form of intaglio.

3. Lithography is printing from a flat surface. It uses greasy material that repels water. When ink and water are applied, the ink sticks to the greasy substance.

4. Serigraphy is any kind of stenciling. *Seri* means silk. Silk screening is a kind of serigraphy.

Look at the explorations from this unit and try to determine which of the four kinds of printmaking each one is.

You need a potato and a carving tool. This is a good project to introduce real artist carving tools, but you can just use a regular old knife too.

Additional Layer

Often the first three or four prints an artist makes of any piece are different than the rest of the edition the artist prints. These first prints are called artist's proofs. They are like the test prints. They are labeled with an "AP" for artist's proof. Often the artist and the printer or others involved in the process get to keep the AP's.

Decide on your design. Cut your potato in half and draw the design on your potato. Cut away everything except the design that you want to show up.

Dip the potato in paint or brush it with ink and stamp onto paper.

😊 🙂 😊 EXPLORATION: Fruit and Veggie Prints
Cut slices off fruits and veggies, dip in ink or paints and press onto paper for interesting patterns.

Additional Layer
You can use vegetable print designs to make holiday or seasonal decorations too. A pumpkin cut in half can make neat painted jack-o-lanterns. Green peppers make great shamrocks for St. Patrick's day. Lettuce can make giant spring flowers.

What else can you make?

☺ ☻ EXPLORATION: Linoleum Print

You need a piece of linoleum and sharp cutting tools to carve a design with. There is a product called softoleum which was created for kids as the surface is easy to cut into.   The cutters are specifically for carving prints and can be found at craft supply stores. Once your design is carved, you ink the surface, put a piece of paper on it, and press the paper down to make your print.

☺ ☻ EXPLORATION: Graphic Designer

Use any graphic design program, from Paint to Illustrator and everything in between, to create a unique digital design you like. You can print it yourself on to paper, or you can submit it to a T-shirt shop and have it silk screened on a bag, shirt, or whatever you'd like. There are online stores that will make it for you inexpensively. I found lots for less than $10, and that includes the shirt. I've shown one that I designed with one of my favorite little sayings.

☺ ☻ ☻ EXPLORATION: Yarn Stamp

Yarn wrapped around a wood block makes a really neat stamp. You can wrap it in many different ways. If the wood is cut into other shapes and then wrapped, you'll have even more looks. Just dip it lightly into tempera or acrylic paints and press on to paper.

☺ ☻ ☻ EXPLORATION: What is a Print?

Go visit this website where you can watch and learn all about prints and printmaking:
http://www.moma.org/interactives/projects/2001/whatisaprint/flash.html

---

On The Web
Read about how this lady made inexpensive frames to do silk screening with her kids, then try it yourself.
http://onegoldenapple.blogspot.com/2009/05/simple-silk-screening-with-kids-or-not.html

Additional Layer
Simply using a stencil is one kind of printmaking. Buy a stencil, or make your own using heavy card stock, and create multiple designs.

American artist Amanda Marie does all her art with stencils.

Fabulous Facts
Once a certain number of prints are made, the plate they were made from is destroyed so no one can print more later.

At the bottom of a print a few things are written in pencil: a fraction (like 12/25, which means that the print is number twelve of a total of twenty five prints made from one plate), a title, the artist's name, and sometimes the date.

Additional Layer

The fewer prints an artist makes of a particular piece, the more expensive each one tends to be. If anyone can easily get one, it's not worth nearly as much as if they are rare.

Some states have laws that say you can only print so many copies before the work is considered a commercial poster instead of fine art.

Writer's Workshop

Here is *The Scream* by Edvard Munch. How is that man feeling? What do you think happened to him? Make up a story about his tragedy and write it in your writer's notebook.

☺ ☺ ☺ EXPLORATION: Rolling Pin Printing

Attach foam stickers all over a rolling pin, then roll in a paint tray or apply paint with a foam brush and then on to paper or solid colored fabric. If you want multiple colors in your design you should definitely use a foam brush. You can make a giant version of this using a cardboard mailing tube as your rolling pin. The added bonus is that once your project is all done you can just throw away the paint-smeared mailing tube and avoid a lot of cleaning up paint.

☺ ☺ ☺ EXPLORATION: Glitter Glue Symmetry Prints

This is an easy project even for little ones. Fold a piece of construction paper in half creating a crease down the center. Make a design on one side using glitter pens or glitter glue. You can do this with regular paint too, but the glitter just makes it even more fun. When the design is done, fold the paper in half again, open it back up, and your design will have created a second symmetrical design on the other side. You can just make abstract markings, or you can create a picture or scene. Here is one with fireworks:

☺ ☺ ☺ EXPLORATION: Leaf Printing

Try this easy printing technique. Get some large, sturdy leaves and paint on the veiny side with tempera paints. You can use a variety of colors and any patterns you like. When the leaves are painted, press them on to paper. You can do it several times before you need to reload your paint. Create beautiful, colorful leaf prints.

☺ ☺ ☺ EXPLORATION: Monoprint Screams

Look at the picture of Edvard Munch's *The Scream* for inspiration while you do this printing project. Now take a flattened piece of sturdy clay and use sharp tools to carve out the shape of a normal face in the clay. Once your face is done, stretch the clay out to manipulate the way the face looks, like how the face on *The Scream* looks elongated. Now use a foam brush to apply paint to the carved side of the clay and print it on to a sheet of paper. You can press the paper down on the clay if that's easier.

😊 😊 EXPLORATION: Durer's Woodcut Prints

Albrect Durer was a German artist who was kind of the quintessential printmaker. He carved designs into soft wood, inked the surface, then pressed wet paper on to it to transfer the ink design. The same woodcut carving could be used over and over again to make many prints. He wasn't the only artist to do this, but he is probably the best known. He made beautiful and intricate prints like the one at the beginning of this section and *The Rhinoceros* from the sidebar.

You can create woodcut prints exactly as Durer did. Gather a variety of metal objects, a hammer, and a piece of soft wood (ask at a home improvement store). You may also need a cloth if the wood is very soft.

1. Place one of the metal objects on top of the wood and pound it with the hammer so it leaves an impression in the wood. You can put a cloth over the pieces so the hammer doesn't leave a mark.
2. Continue to hammer and make impressions until you are happy with your design. Nails make dots, screwdrivers make lines. Look around the garage or shed and see what other metal objects you can find that would make interesting indentations.
3. When you're ready to make your print, cover the top surfaces of wood with ink or paint using an ink pad or foam brush with paint. Don't get any in the cracks you've carved.
4. Place a sheet of paper on top of the wood and rub hard with your fingers all over the design so the whole thing transfers. Be careful not to let it slip or move while your printing. Pull the paper up and take a look at your design.

Coming up next . . .
Unit 2-13
African Kingdoms
Mali
Carbon Chemistry
Textiles

My Ideas For This Unit:

Title: _____   Topic: _____

_____
_____
_____
_____
_____
_____
_____
_____
_____

Title: _____   Topic: _____

_____
_____
_____
_____
_____
_____
_____
_____
_____
_____

Title: _____   Topic: _____

_____
_____
_____
_____
_____
_____
_____
_____
_____

Eastern Europe: Unit 2-12

895   2-12
Magyars begin to settle Carpathian Basin

955   2-12
Germans beat Magyar invaders, stopping the raids across Europe

1001   2-12
Pope recognizes Christian Kingdom of Hungary, Stephen is king

1212   2-12
Golden Bull founds Kingdom of Bohemia

1217   2-12
Serbian Kingdom proclaimed and established

1224-1239   2-12
Teutonic Knights conquer Prussians

1237   2-12
Mongols begin to invade Russia

1241   2-12
Mongols invade Poland and Hungary

1242   2-12
Russians defeat Teutonic Knights at Lake Peipus

1342   2-12
Death of Gedymin, founder of Lithuania

1355-1378   2-12
Charles IV of Bohemia reigns as Holy Roman Emperor

1362   2-12
Battle of Blue Waters, Lithuanians beat the Golden Horde, giving Lithuania control over Kiev

1386   2-12
Poland and Lithuania united through marriage

1389   2-12
Battle of Kosovo, Ottomans defeat and control Balkans

1410   2-12
Teutonic Knights defeated at the battle of Tannenberg (Grunwald) by a Polish-Lithuanian alliance

1526   2-12
Ottomans defeat Hungarians at the Battle of Mohacs and then begin to occupy much of Eastern Europe

Norway

Sweden

Finland
(controlled by Sweden)

Denmark

☆ Battle of
Lake Peipus

• Konigsburg

• Danzig

• Berlin
• Frankfurt

• Kiev

Holy Roman
Empire

• Cracow

Khanate of the Golden Horde

Italy

•Belgrade

Eastern
Europe
c. 1400 AD

☆ Battle of
Kosovo

Constantinople

Byzantine Empire

• Athens

Transylvania
In Hungary During the Middle Ages

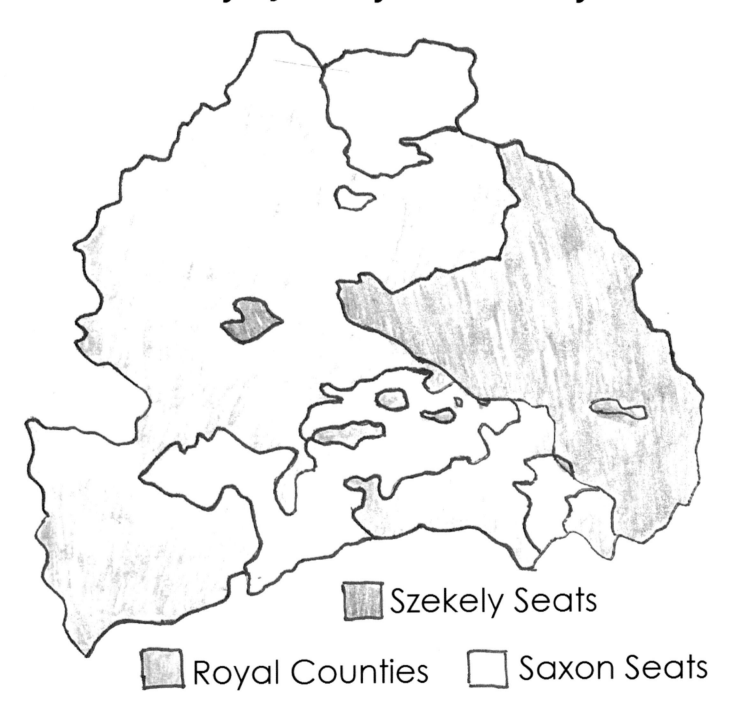

▨ Szekely Seats

▨ Royal Counties ☐ Saxon Seats

Hungarian Stag Strap

This is what an actual strap end from a Medieval Hungarian horse harness looked like. It was worked in silver metal. Color it, paste it onto cardboard, and cut it out.

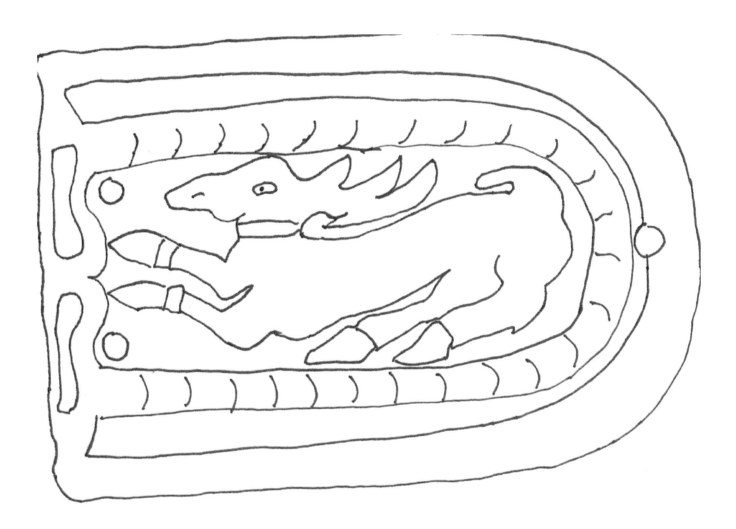

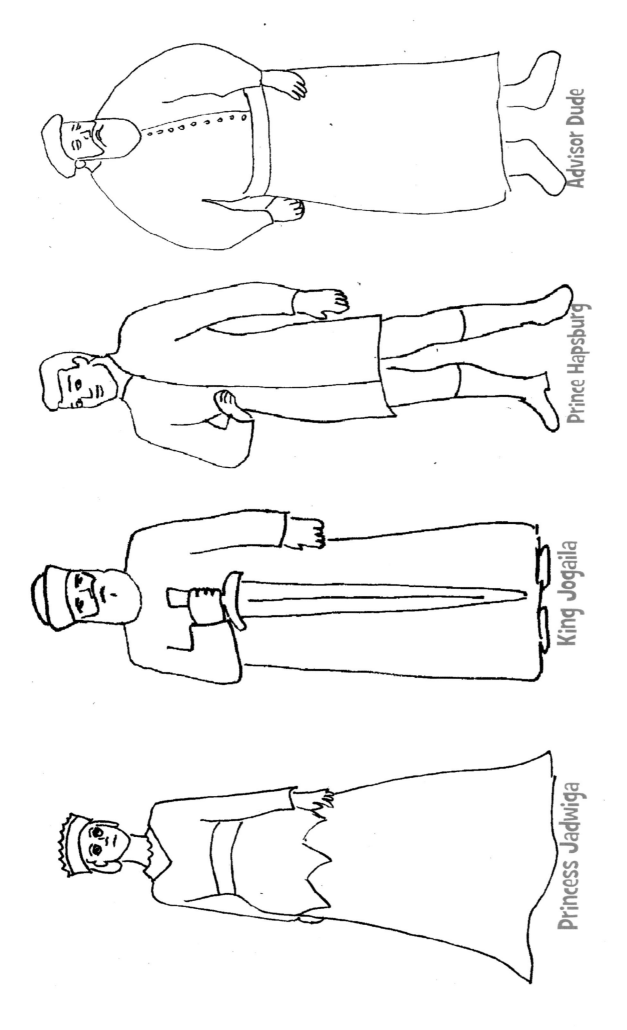

Advisor Dude

Prince Hapsburg

King Jogaila

Princess Jadwiga

Periodic Table of the Elements

Group 1	2	3	4	5	6	7	8	9	10	11	12	13	14	15	16	17	18
1 H Hydrogen 1.0																	2 He Helium 4.0
3 Li Lithium 6.9	4 Be Beryllium 9.0											5 B Boron 10.8	6 C Carbon 12.0	7 N Nitrogen 14.0	8 O Oxygen 16.0	9 F Fluorine 19.0	10 Ne Neon 20.2
11 Na Sodium 23.0	12 Mg Magnesium 24.3											13 Al Aluminum 27.0	14 Si Silicon 28.1	15 P Phosphorus 31.0	16 S Sulfur 32.1	17 Cl Chlorine 35.5	18 Ar Argon 40.0
19 K Potassium 39.1	20 Ca Calcium 40.1	21 Sc Scandium 45.0	22 Ti Titanium 47.9	23 V Vanadium 50.9	24 Cr Chromium 52.0	25 Mn Manganese 54.9	26 Fe Iron 55.9	27 Co Cobalt 58.9	28 Ni Nickel 58.7	29 Cu Copper 63.5	30 Zn Zinc 65.4	31 Ga Gallium 69.7	32 Ge Germanium 72.6	33 As Arsenic 74.9	34 Se Selenium 79.0	35 Br Bromine 79.9	36 Kr Krypton 83.8
37 Rb Rubidium 85.5	38 Sr Strontium 87.6	39 Y Yttrium 88.9	40 Zr Zirconium 91.2	41 Nb Niobium 92.9	42 Mo Molybdenum 95.9	43 Tc Technetium 99	44 Ru Ruthenium 101.0	45 Rh Rhodium 102.9	46 Pd Palladium 106.4	47 Ag Silver 107.9	48 Cd Cadmium 112.4	49 In Indium 114.8	50 Sn Tin 118.7	51 Sb Antimony 121.8	52 Te Tellurium 127.6	53 I Iodine 126.9	54 Xe Xenon 131.3
55 Cs Cesium 132.9	56 Ba Barium 137.3	Lanthanides 57-71	72 Hf Hafnium 178.5	73 Ta Tantalum 180.9	74 W Tungsten 183.9	75 Re Rhenium 186.2	76 Os Osmium 190.2	77 Ir Iridium 192.2	78 Pt Platinum 195.1	79 Au Gold 197.0	80 Hg Mercury 200.6	81 Tl Thallium 204.4	82 Pb Lead 207.2	83 Bi Bismuth 209.0	84 Po Polonium 210.0	85 At Astatine 211	86 Rn Radon 222.0
87 Fr Francium 223.0	88 Ra Radium 226.0	Actinides 89-103	104 Rf Rutherfordium 267	105 Db Dubnium 268	106 Sg Seaborgium 271	107 Bh Bohrium 272	108 Hs Hassium 270	109 Mt Meitnerium 276	110 Ds Darmstadtium 281	111 Rg Roentgenium 280	112 Cn Copernicium 285	113 Uut Ununtrium 284	114 Fl Flerovium 289	115 Uup Ununpentium 288	116 Lv Livermorium 293	117 Uus Ununseptium 294	118 Uuo Ununoctium 294

Lanthanides

57 La Lanthanum 138.9	58 Ce Cerium 140.1	59 Pr Praseodymium 140.9	60 Nd Neodymium 144.2	61 Pm Promethium 145	62 Sm Samarium 150.4	63 Eu Europium 152.0	64 Gd Gadolinium 157.3	65 Tb Terbium 158.9	66 Dy Dysprosium 162.5	67 Ho Holmium 164.0	68 Er Erbium 167.3	69 Tm Thulium 168.9	70 Yb Ytterbium 173.0	71 Lu Lutetium 175.0

Actinides

89 Ac Actinium 227.0	90 Th Thorium 232.0	91 Pa Protactinium 231.0	92 U Uranium 238.0	93 Np Neptunium 237	94 Pu Plutonium 242	95 Am Americium 243	96 Cm Curium 247	97 Bk Berkelium 247	98 Cf Californium 251	99 Es Einsteinium 254	100 Fm Fermium 253	101 Md Mendelevium 256	102 No Nobelium 254	103 Lr Lawrencium 257

Angels and Christmas Trees

In Hungary the children can't wait for Christmas Eve. They say an angel comes to their house and brings them a beautifully decorated tree just in time for Christmas. Draw the decorated Christmas tree this angel brought.